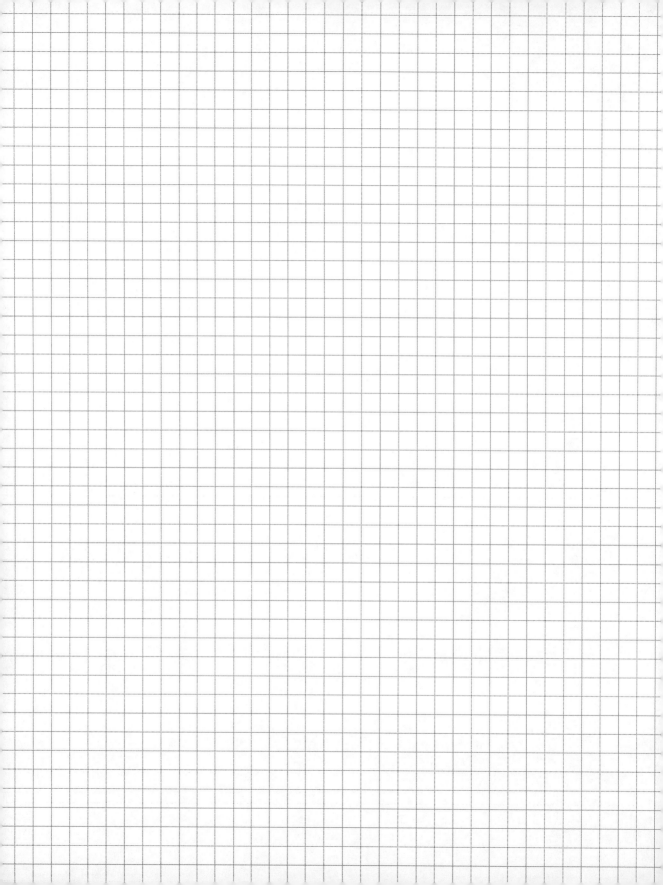

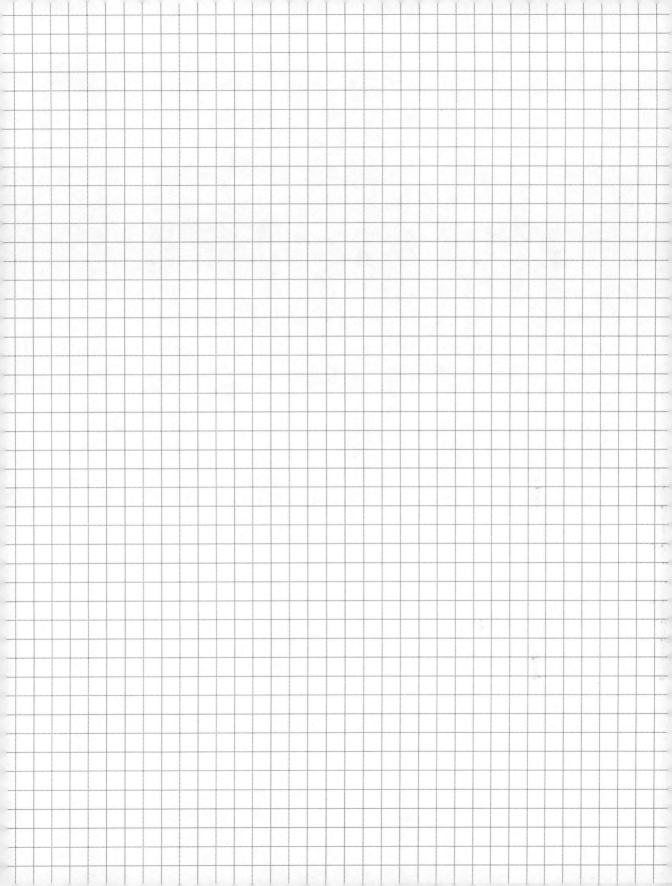

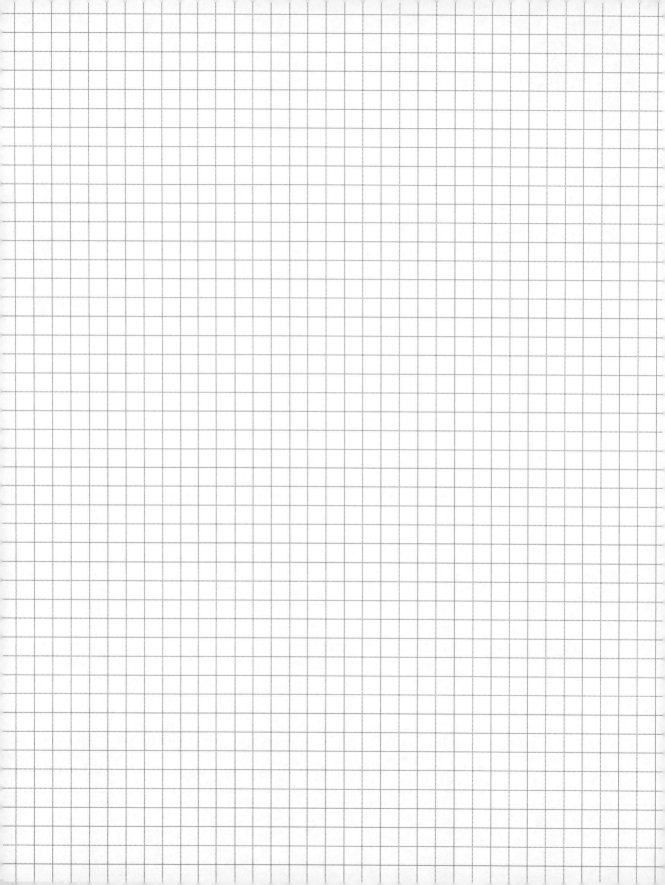

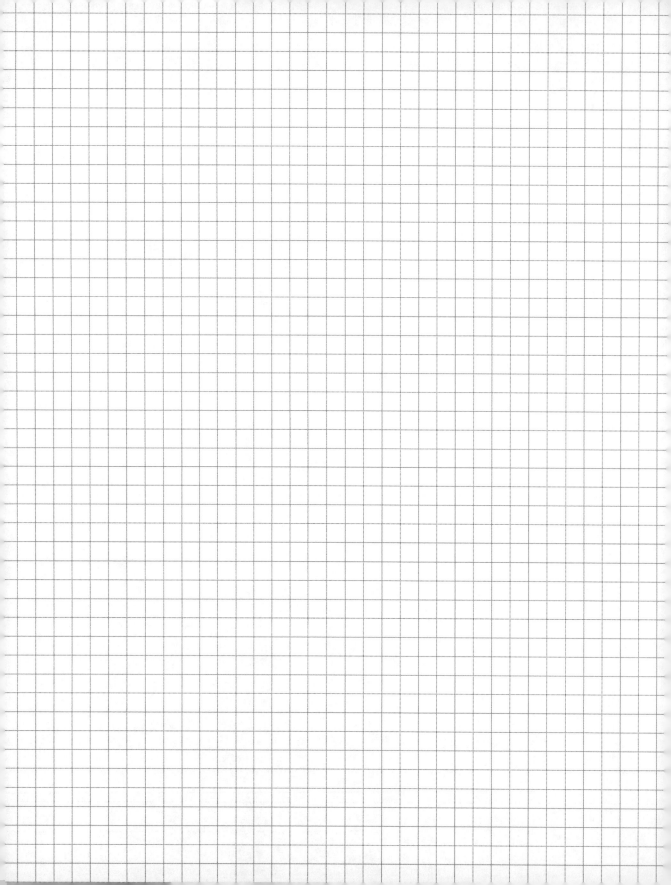

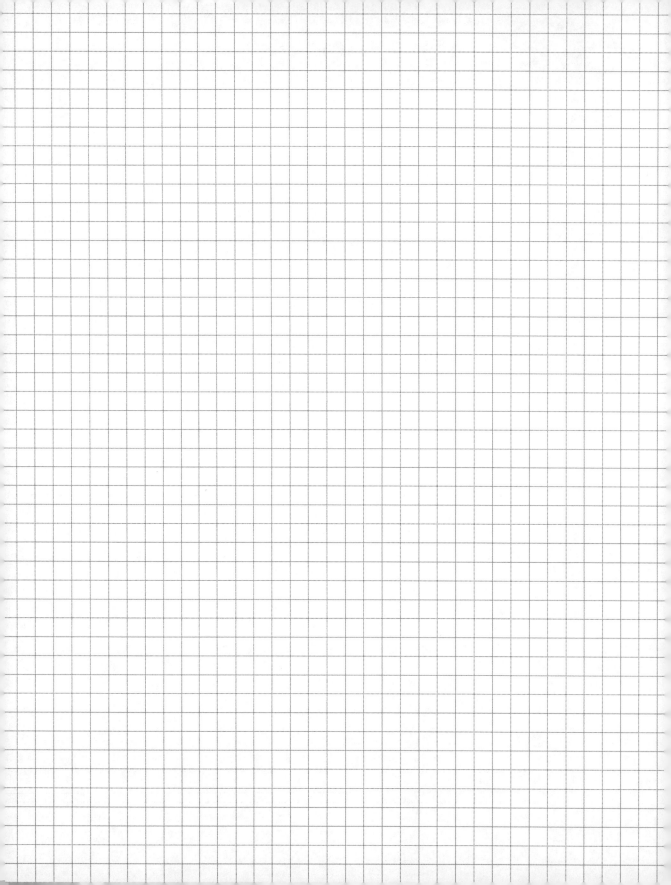

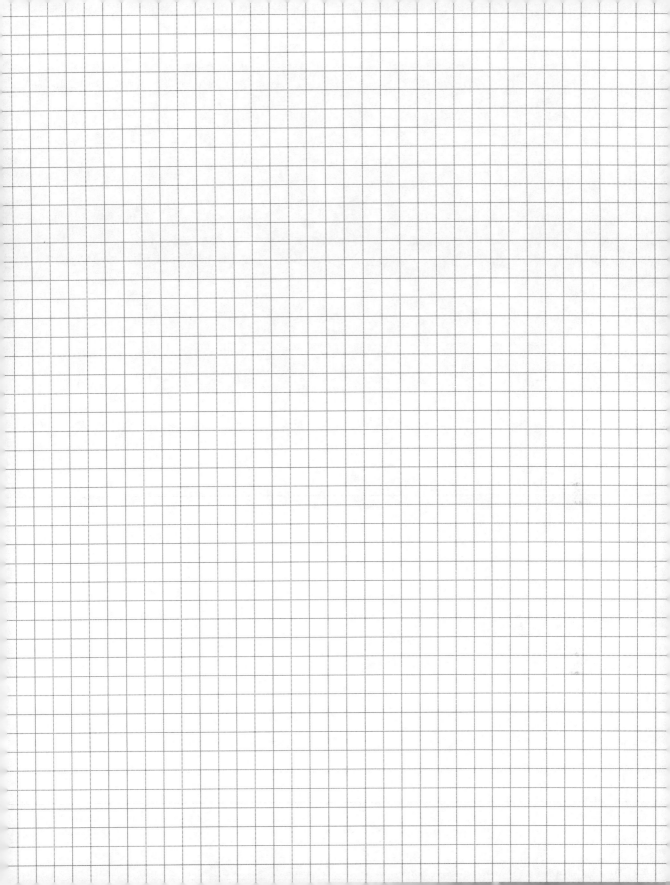

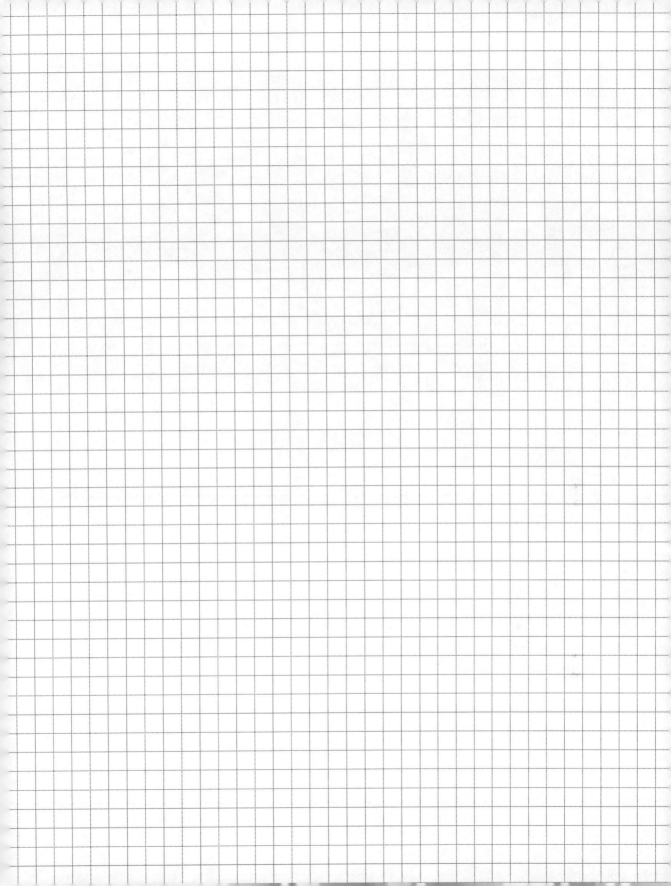

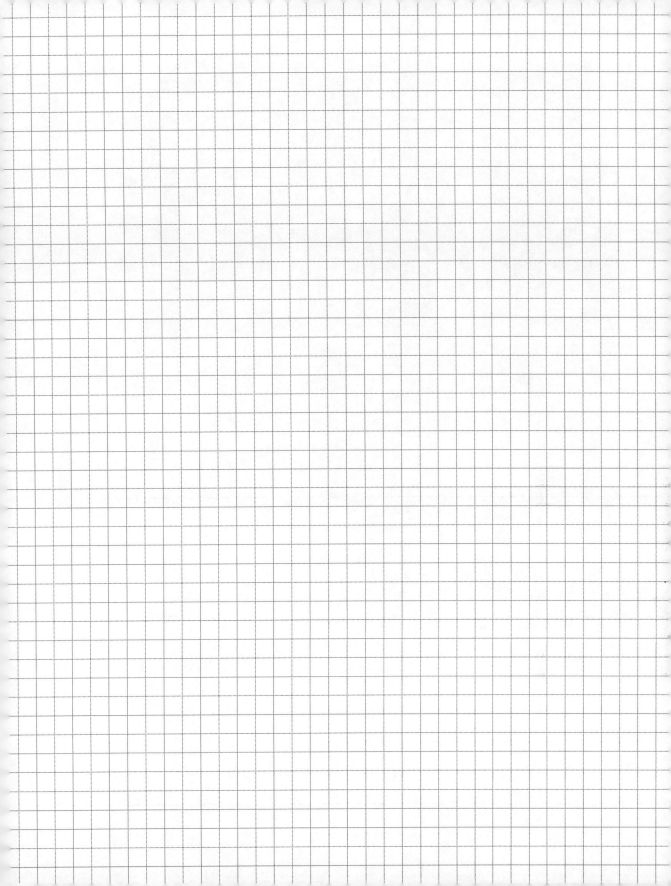

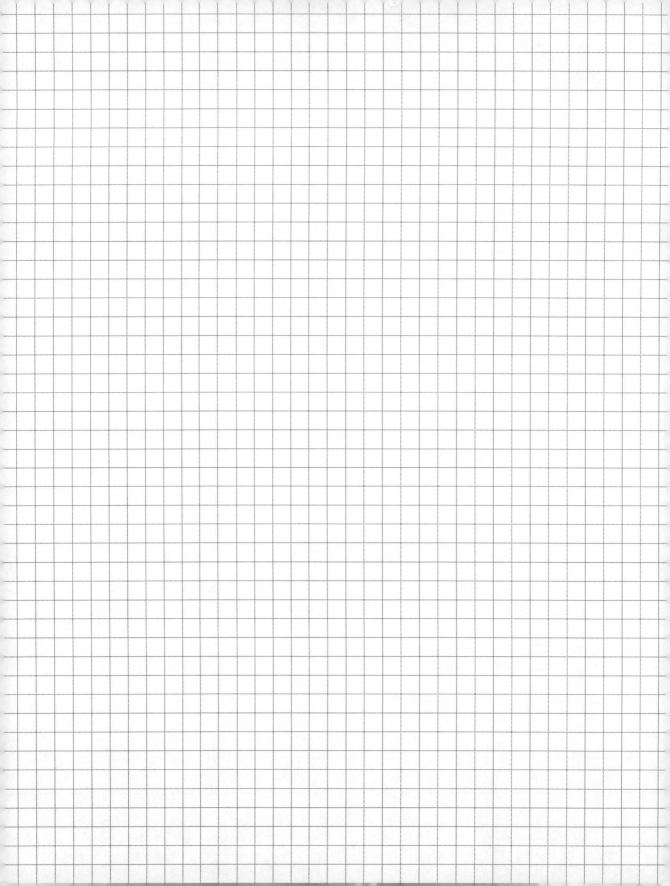

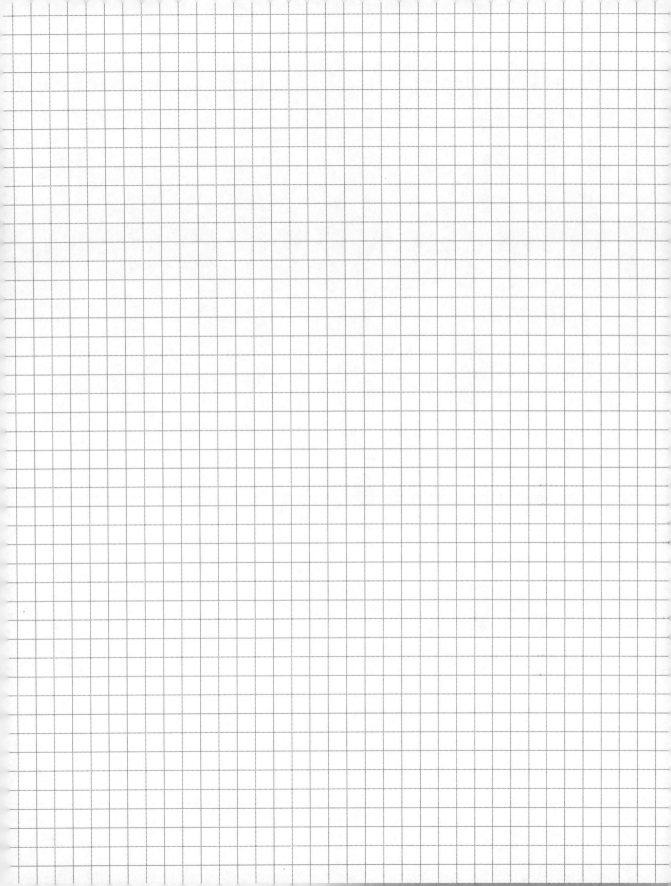

Made in the USA
Las Vegas, NV
14 April 2024

88690216R00065